.aise for Jim Daniels

"Jim Daniels keeps getting better, going deeper into his lived life to find there the language of celebration, lamentation, victory, defeat, moral ambiguity, and political and social outrage. He curses what needs to be cursed, he blesses what needs to be blessed, and he stands in silent awe and wonder at the world turning about him, a world of unaccountable suffering and unaccounted for beauty. And while that world resists Daniels's best efforts to be made sense of, complex as it is, giant as it is, it can't help but yield its music to his gifted mind and impassioned heart."
—Li-Young Lee

"Daniels has the rare ability to combine clarity with sophistication. He captures, as few contemporary poets do, the sounds of North American city speech, illuminating our everyday experiences in the common tongue."
—Julia Stein, *The Village Voice*

"Jim Daniels . . . brings us sad, acutely-observed stories of people who know in their bones that the American Dream does not apply to them."
—John Sayles

"[Jim Daniels's] poems . . . have sung of our daily existence, the lives of the suburban and urban, the family and the loner, the lovers and losers, the workers and the unemployed. And contained inside these songs are our most pressing moral and philosophical issues, in language as it exists in the larger culture, the hot breath of the world-right-now, and also in a voice, across fourteen collections of poems, that [he's] somehow made all [his] own—the necessary contradiction, I think, for any great writer."
—Justin Bigos, *32 Poems Magazine*

Praise for Jim Daniels

"As with the best poetry, one can read Jim Daniels on many levels. Not to read him at all is to miss a most important and original contemporary."
—Robert McDowell, *The Hudson Review*

"There is a melancholy sweetness running through these poems that, while not entirely redemptive, offers unexpected relief and enables us to see that Jim Daniels, despite the tough-bitten talk, is a poet born to praise."
—Carol Muske, *New York Times Book Review*

"Staring into the past can be perilous, but Jim Daniels can stand on the slopes of nostalgia without slipping. With *In Line for the Exterminator*, it must be his accurate eye and the way we can hear him talking to us in the living present of these poems."
—Billy Collins

"*Eight Mile High*—read that any way you'd like—is a perceptive and sympathetic portrait of a place we don't often hear about from deep inside. Not Detroit, not the affluent suburbs — instead we see young kids trapped in between, stoned, floating on a river of beer; their parents whose lives on the line did not turn out to be as ideal as they seemed now that the old times are gone; and girls and women, for whom the word 'fulfillment' hardly exists. Jim Daniels's people are candid about their disappointments, with here and there a moment of tender contemplation. This is a wonderful book, Daniels's best, so clearly a labor of intense and complicated feeling."
—Rosellen Brown, author of *Before and After and Half a Heart*

"Place grounds us so much in how we generate writing, how we explore our words, how we articulate the home in us. Daniels reminds us not to forget how home builds us forward. . . . This book is about home."
—*Passages North*

ROWING INLAND

MADE IN MICHIGAN WRITERS SERIES

A complete listing of the books in this series can be found online at wsupress.wayne.edu

ROWING INLAND

POEMS BY

JIM DANIELS

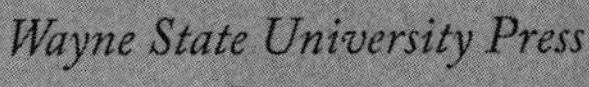
Wayne State University Press

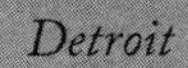
Detroit

21 20 19 18 17 5 4 3 2 1

Library of Congress Control Number: 2016955736

ISBN: 978-0-8143-4218-3 (paperback)
ISBN: 978-0-8143-4219-0 (ebook)

Publication of this book was made possible by a generous gift from The Meijer Foundation. Additional support provided by Michigan Council for Arts and Cultural Affairs and National Endowment for the Arts.

Designed and typeset by Rachel Ross
Composed in Adobe Caslon

Wayne State University Press
Leonard N. Simons Building
4809 Woodward Avenue
Detroit, Michigan 48201-1309

Visit us online at wsupress.wayne.edu

Contents

2. Welcome to Warren

3. Late Invocation for Magic

4. Economic Fairy Tale

Acknowledgments

The Alembic: "Reading Dante's Inferno on Break at Ford's"

Anti-Poetry: "Late Invocation for Magic"

Artful Dodge: "Wishbone"

Big Muddy: "Crooked Teeth"

Blue Collar Review: "Quitting the Day Job in the Middle Ages"

Come Together: Imagine Peace: "Something Like a Sonnet for Something Like Peace"

Corridors: "Economic Fairy Tale: The Cement House"

Crab Creek Review: "Calling Out Marlene Miller"

Crab Orchard Review: "The Monkees, 1968"

Crazyhorse: "Dead Girl"

DMQ Review: "Customs"

Diode: "Family Relics: The Suicide Policeman's Blackjack"

Ducts: "Last Meals"

Dunes Review: "The End of Childhood," "Around the Block"

Fail Better: "The Exploding Cigar Tour"

The Florida Review: "A Game Called Rock"

The Fox Chase Review: "The St. Vitus Dance of the Factory Floor"

Green Mountains Review: "Infamous"

Harvard Review: "Soft Side of the Moon"

Hiram Poetry Review: "My Mother Recalls the Miracle of the Loaf (No Fish)"

Hotel Amerika: "Letter to Andy"

Hubbub: "Easter Sunday at Hakim's Convenience," "Summer Weight, Labor Day"

Jabberwock: "Talking by the Fence"

The Louisville Review: "Prayer above the Washer"

Map Literary: "Second Shift Closed the Bar"

Moon City Review: "*Three Sonnets:* Cutting My Grandfather's Grass"

Natural Bridge: "Beware of (*My Grandfather's Fake*) Dog"

Passages North: "Hard Candy"

The Paterson Literary Review: "Swiss Steak," "Home Improvement," "Legendary Parks," "Homemade Prom Dress"

A Peculiar History of Detroit: "Photo of My Grandparents Working Their Lunch Wagon at the Gates of Dodge Main"

Poet Lore: "The Heavy Stuff," "Christmas Dinner, 2008"

Poetry Northwest: "Crayola Trailer Park Eight-Pack"

Postcard Poems and Prose: "Painting a Picture with Broken Crayons"

Red Rock Review: "Laughing from Here," "FOE: Forwarding Order Expired," "Rowing Inland"

Slipstream: "Room Divider"

The Southampton Review: "'School's Out,' Alice Cooper, 1972"

The Spillway Review: "Homeless Arisen from Dead"

Toasted Cheese: "Weeding Out the Weak"

Tygerburning: "The Unpregnant Pause"

Work: "Rouge Overpass"

World Literature Today: "Hidden Beauty"

The Xavier Review: "July 20 Fireworks During Ongoing Conflicts Abroad"

Customs

Impossible to get lost on the long, straight roads in/around/through Detroit, yet we tried, punks brash with stubborn loneliness, even in cars packed tight. From Six Mile Road out to—where did they stop?—32, 38 Mile Road? Each a mile apart, and the crossroads—Ryan, Dequindre, Mound, Van Dyke—all a mile apart. Driving those streets like playing Dots and Boxes, where you connect dots till whoever forms a box writes their initials inside. Inevitably, we traced boxes, driving our cranky, rusty beasts, turning right, left. We always knew where we were, that all the boxes were ours and none of them were, and so we could not write any initials—if we plunged down a side street, it was like holding our heads under water. In less than a mile or minute, we'd surface and know our exact location.

So the freeways drew us in, I-75, I-94, I-96, I-696—twisting over and under street grids, rivers fast and rivers dangerous, roaring with the rapids of our engines—whoosh/whoosh/whoosh—past each other, making wind in the night under the silent glow of the fixed stars lining pavement. And some reckless nights, we could end up on a bridge or in a tunnel and arrive in Canada to answer questions about who we were and where we were going.

1

ROWING INLAND

Home Improvement

My father built a basement bedroom
for the two oldest boys. Brown linoleum,
two-by-fours, paneling, ceiling tiles—

hours scraped from rock between work
and work—Christmas, a week each summer,
one weekend a month. For seven years—
one hammer rising and falling—one room.

This summer, I painted my porch roof,
splattering white onto the tree below
till it resembled work by an obscure
modern artist. My children danced beneath me—
back off, I shouted from the shaky ladder.

My father had two cancerous moles removed,
to my disbelief—he never saw the sun.
Five children against the wall, squirming
for the camera, for the missing father.

The paneling hides the strike zone
I drew on cement in crayon. Will anyone
ever uncover it and fire another fastball?

Ceiling and walls remain half-finished,
a patchwork of rec room and cellar.
I run my hands over the edges
where he stopped. My mother
can no longer descend the steps
despite the double railing installed
thirty years ago for her own mother.

He does the laundry now. Light sifts
down through glass-block windows.
He worked for Ford's for 33 years.
He sometimes laughs now. I do not want
to stray far from my mother's voice
asking me to bring something up for her.
She steadies herself on the landing.

Upstairs, she kept the order.
Downstairs, he drove another nail in.

Rowing Inland

On the only vacation of my childhood
we followed the Detroit legend of "Great Lakes,
Great Times" up the gridlock of I-75 to a cottage
in the holy expanse we called Up North.

On Tea Lake, where I never saw anyone drink tea
or discuss tea, or remark that the color of the lake
resembled tea, we rented one of the dilapidated shacks
owned by a cousin of our neighbor Branco

and referred to without irony as a resort.
I was rib-boned skinny at ten, and Kim,
Branco's daughter, was nine, blond hair
bleached by that bright young sun.

Our parents drank beer and smoked cigarettes
as always—but longer, with more savor—
in splintery chairs on the splintery dock.
Our fathers discussed fishing but did no fishing.

They shouted to those in rowboats,
how's the fishing? but they did no fishing.
I only faintly began to realize life
was mostly a series of rhetorical questions:

Hot enough for you? Working hard,
or hardly working? Our fathers carried
identical black lunch buckets each morning
to different locations linked by the same underground

tunnel of machinery and grease and one giant time clock
registering the equation of the city's heartbeat
divided by the number of new cars built that year.
Our mothers discussed other mothers and swore

off cooking for a week, swore like they never did
at home. *Shit*, they sighed, *shit*, echoing out over
calm water. Straps on bathing suits hung loose.
They painted their nails because they could.

They lost track of their children. Kim and I sat
in a rotting wooden rowboat on the weedy shore.
We donned faded orange life vests
and placed oars in locks and rowed

through sand and air, calling *stroke, stroke*
like we'd seen in a cartoon about a dog.
We never laughed at cartoons—no one
ever really got hurt. No TV at Tea Lake.

Coffee and beer. We were allowed orange drink
in paper cartons, and potato chips galore.
Left alone, we caught fireflies and poison ivy,
mosquito bites and berries, and firecrackers

from the bad kid down the road who spat
with alarming accuracy. We waded in shallow water,
screwing our feet into cold muck. Roads were dirt,
and street signs nonexistent. We carved our names

on white birch bark and imagined
we had the bravery and stealth of Indians.
After a week, we were back on the grid
of our shallow street, riding the banks of curbs

on our bikes and setting ants on fire.
If you look at anything long and hard enough,
it catches fire. Another giant clock out there:
the Tragedy Clock. No second, minute,

or hour hands. Just a big gong sounding
without warning. One stroke after another
killed her father. He called me Jimmy, limping
out of his pickup, bearing that black, metal coffin

home each day while I sat on her porch or mine.
Kim and I kissed in the realm of first and foremost,
climbing out bedroom windows when we were thirteen.
But we never went to the church of full penetration

and instead slipped away from each other
like embarrassed fish released back to water,
still bloody from the hook. I didn't get anyone
pregnant until I was 23. We had to gas up twice

and cross state lines for the procedure.
Kim left school and married the father.
It didn't sit right with Branco. She moved
away, and I didn't see her for years.

Branco held her child in his wheelchair
the last time I saw either of them. I waved
from my porch. *It's Jimmy*, I said.
Her husband—do you want me to go on,

pounding the Tragedy Clock
with my mallet? *Stroke, stroke,*
we rowed together over the shore.

Swiss Steak

The Burks' kitchen, the first I smelled
that was not my mother's. Tiny houses
squeezed us onto streets, sharing stones,
curses, dares, but not kitchens. Allowed
to stand in doorways or play in basements or use
the bathroom, we never ate in each other's houses.
The Burks, new neighbors, thought their son
Gerard might be my friend.

My mother licked her hand, smoothed
my cowlick and sent me off, a second grader
squinting through winter's steamed glasses.
I trudged through snow in black rubber boots
to a house just like my own. I didn't figure in
odd mixed odors I could not name
hanging in the stifled air of forced smiles.

Swiss steak tasted like betrayal, or at least
some level of lie, as I carefully sliced it,
red gravy seeping into mushy rice, like blood
from the wound of some desanctified saint.

Not the bland body of Christ, though they
recited our same prayer. Not cotton candy
at the school fair. Not the exhaust fan spewing
grease behind Oscar's Award Hamburgers.

Pudding for dessert. I swirled mine into
an eddy. Silence swelled around my slurping.
No dessert at home—dessert for *eight*?
Our cookie jar, a cruel joke.

Mr. Burk wore the tie of someone's boss.
Kitchen windows fogged with the foreign.
I sat mute, marooned, till my mother phoned
and I gladly fled. Perhaps I thanked them,
but I don't think I did.

Wishbone

My mother commanded her kitchen corner—
two casement windows cranked open
in summer while she steamed above
sudsy dishes, her five kids shot
into dusk's after-dinner space—
the street, and other kids like us.

Two potted violets from her dead mother
anchored the sills. If you find my father
in this picture, please let me know.
We still look for him far from that tiny house.
My mother dried wishbones on those sills.
It was she who decided they were dry enough
to break. She never wished herself.

Talking by the Fence

When his brother returned to Greece
for the summer, Nick Mandros moved in next door.
My mother at the sink absently wiped dishes
waiting for Nick to step out. She did a lot of

weeding that summer, leaning over the fence,
laughing till hot gossip melted our Tupperware.
My mother quit Card Club, and good riddance.
She hid in the house till they turned

to Mrs. Fiore in her gold metal-flake bikini
lying in the sun with cigarette and drink
and the funkiest sunglasses ever seen on Rome Street,
sometimes hiding a black eye from Mr. Fiore.

Mrs. Fiore told them to *fuck off*
when Mr. Todd with his lawn-care truck
and slick, oily smile, parked out front,
slipped inside and stayed for hours.

Nick made my mother smile and laugh
in ways my father had not time for—a gray absence
trudging up the dark drive after work to collapse
with a cigarette sigh. Once, at the end of the summer,

Nick leaned against the fence to ask about my mother.

I dropped my ball then picked it up. I looked back

at the open kitchen window. *How's your mom*,

he asked again. I kicked at spreading weeds.

Fine, I answered, *fine*.

Three Sonnets: Cutting My Grandfather's Grass

when he could no longer.
Rusty gas can spilled into dust.
Yank yank yank till the engine caught.

He squirmed in a rusted porch chair in his straw fedora
as if he had to go, as if he had something to say
but—*but but but butbutbut.*

In his dank basement, all the world's tools
sat clean and oiled and ready to march while their leader
sat idle outside, sweating into his yellow handkerchief.

He kept a skunky beer in his fridge for such occasions.
Back and forth—the mower shot up the occasional rock
at which he'd nod. Perhaps acknowledging

life's unexpected projectiles. He pinned a twenty
to the inside of his shirt to elude muggers.

. . .

The blade plastered grass against the underside of the mower.
The sweet poison of gas and cut grass created waves
of hallucinatory possibilities there in the middle of Detroit

flanked by two vacant lots of rubble.
Just one beer, always, *with your name on it.*
Dandelions and dust, but he wanted it cut.
Perhaps he was sending a message to an obscure holy man—

St. Turfinfinger, patron saint of broken harps.
He had one in his hallway, donated by the abandoned church

across the street. I choked down the beer.
We talked about a trapeze artist he once knew
or the Proving Grounds at Packard where he tested

a 10,000-cylinder engine and ended up on an abandoned planet
very similar to the very spot on which he sat.

. . .

He called me *Jimmy*, and no one else did.
So the day he called me *Boy*, I knew what patch
of grass he was headed for. Damn it, *Boy*, he called me.

I wanted the street to know he had a strong young man
looking out for him, more real than the fake dog
he conjured with appropriate signage,

dog house, bones, and bowls. When I drove
away, he waved till I was out of sight,
and I did the same for him.

Ah, gasoline. Ah, cut grass. A small patch,
sneeze of green on the dusty gray street. Two
of his own children had died in that house.

I always missed a spot so it looked more
like somebody lived there.

Beware of (*My Grandfather's Fake*) Dog

His shrunken street, tight with menace and doubt,
his busted jaw and memory bank, convinced us
to move him out. We got him a real dog
for his new house—Jessie, who he spoiled
with pancakes and hot dogs boiled
or raw, and shared meals-on-wheels.

My brothers and I loaded a borrowed truck
while he snuck things off the trash pile
for luck or nostalgia or fear of losing
his entire life story: the ripped-out phone,
a bald tire, broken TV, butter knife. The fake
dog's life he'd staged for imagined safety
stayed behind, guarding the back porch.

Its fake shit, fake bones "gnawed" by scissors,
its red plastic bowls, its thick chain snaking
through the muddy yard. The silence
of its faithful bark faded as we fled in the dark.

Prayer Above the Washer

Sunlight through basement glass block
above cement washtubs, and a bare bulb
dim against the new day. I listen
to my mother's muted shuffle above me.
She's sent me down to find something,
bring it back up. I scratch my nails into a bar
of cracked yellow soap. They have just sold
this house of my childhood. I read the prayer
she taped beneath the window. Should it too
be removed, packed? I conjure ghosted piles
of laundry, the fifty-pound detergent barrels
I sulked on, swigging warm beer
from my father's cases stacked under the stairs.
Her voice calls down to me, "Don't forget . . ."
but in this dim, gentle light,
I am already gone.

My Mother Recalls the Miracle of the Loaf (No Fish)

Winter, and my father was dead. My mother
worked for nuns for next to nothing.
Nothing itself lurked outside. Black ice,
dim futures. Whiskers of exhaust
flecked the roadside snow, and I sang,
Fa-ther, fa-ther against the clouded glass.
She sent me to Charlie's Market down
the block, pressing extra silver into
my tender palm, curling my fingers
around it: *Fresh*, she said, so soft
I had to ask again. And repeat
at the counter, Charlie's dour wife
disbelieving. *I know your mother*,
she said, *she only gets day-old.* True
enough. *But*, I said. *But she said*, I said.
Mrs. Charlie, we called her, and she didn't
seem to mind, though she too had a name.
They'd started to call your grandmother
Widow McLaird. I brought the nothing home
to her angry tears. I watched the little ones
while she stormed back to fetch the fresh.

She sliced the loaf that night at dinner—
soup, it was, watery broth from a bone.
Your Uncle Pat complained the bread
was *too soft*. She smiled her sadness then
at me, for we shared a secret. I, the oldest,
the only one left to understand.

I know now what to label that loaf
warm with the smell of bittersweet.
Not French or Italian. Not rye
or pumpernickel. I almost wished
that I wasn't old enough for irony.
The Day-Old Family, I called us
to myself, to make me smile
from then ever after. I wish I knew
what made her splurge that day.
Fresh, she whispered. *Fresh*.

Photo of My Grandparents Working Their Lunch Wagon at the Gates of Dodge Main

Their signs guard the wagon with the sincerity
of hand-painted lettering. The grunge and grumble
of factory workers raggedly straggle into one more line
in their lined lives. My grandmother's scarved head pokes
into the photo from behind my grandfather's
stooped bulk. He takes the money. She cooks.
Depression took their corner store, my grandfather's
charm losing currency. The guys in line have
no time for his inflated tales of the war-to-end-them-all.
They eye the sky's time clock, the tiny spark
of my grandmother, or just the plain ground.
They must know the world's rigged against them.
My grandfather's hand, extended, waits forever.

Family Relics: The Suicide Policeman's Blackjack

I look for bloodstains in the leather
like I looked for Lincoln's in the chair
from Ford's Theater roped off in Greenfield Village
to imagine the moment of impact.

He killed himself with his *service revolver*,
the brittle clipping reads. Small enough
to miss in the daily paper
but someone didn't.

My great uncle. I got his watch fixed.
Won for racing pigeons, it hangs
on its ceremonial hook as if waiting
to hypnotize the naïve or compassionate.

The blackjack, the clipping, the watch.
You might think it a mysterious triangle
but we follow dotted lines, jump over the gaps
in the liquored pools of our besotted history.

. . .

My father enters the frame
turns the scrapbook page
fingers the blackjack
whacks the loose ball bearings
in their dry leather sack against his palm,
another way we keep time
in our family

and I'm hearing shot glasses
clocking against the wooden table
in a rhythmic dirge
some might blame on blood

so who did he hit and when,
and why are there no survivors
to smudge these pages,
to fill in and erase and reinvent,
to claim the watch
to claim the blackjack
and its history of hitting?

. . .

I stared at the leather chair
roped off from my grasp
and imagined the dark, stuffy theater
and the enormous Lincoln of history books.

I listen to my father enumerate the victims
of the curse that runs—does not walk
or stroll or jog or mosey—in the family.
The particulars, I imagine.

The bedtime story I half-told myself
in my own drunken years—
good uncles, great cousins, aunts,
laughter cut short, watch hands woozy.

We changed the spelling of our name
and the labels on our bottles.
We hid the weapons and the maps.
The keys and the locks.

. . .

My father flutters the pages
and I hear the wings
of pigeons, the dirty birds
of our heritage.
By his own hand. Somewhere
a steady hand fixed the watch
while cruelty landed its blows
and my father taught me
not to turn away
but to witness
and pass on.

The blackjack in a box
will be mine,
the rhythm section to the song
I sing to my children
about the small dogs of their dreams
that do not bark or bite
about the birds who come home to roost
and how we shoo them away
by all means necessary.
About how I define survival
as avoiding small hard things and reading
small print, and telling time
the old-fashioned way.

Second Shift Closed the Bar

putting the sea back together

after Moses parted it.

We closed the bar

like dogs done sniffing

each other's butts.

We closed the bar

like eliminated game-show contestants.

We closed the bar

like a rock and a hard place.

We closed the bar

like father, son, and Holy Ghost.

We closed the bar

like the rabbi, the priest, and the transvestite.

We closed the bar

like monkeys waving upside-down sale signs.

We closed the bar

our heads tilted back, inhaling stars.

We closed the bar

like bad report cards.

We closed the bar

like magicians pulling other magicians out of our hats.

We closed the bar

and the bartender was grateful.

We closed the bar

and night air smelled like church smoke.

We closed the bar

and gravel in the parking lot applauded.

We closed the bar
and the clock let down its guard.
We closed the bar
and the half-cocked moon nevertheless took away the keys.
We closed the bar
and we took credit where credit was morning dew.
We closed the bar
and sang the song "Remember the Time"
and made up all the words
and told each other they were true
and the refrain was our breathing,
visible in the cold, under floodlights,
and we rocked our way home
under vicious waves of lullaby.

Reading Dante's Inferno on Break at Ford's

I'd never read it before, and I felt I should—
circles of hell, and I wanted to know which one
was mine. Twenty-one, all about *me*, soft tiny dot
among thick steel blocks of machines,
a smudge easily erased from the picture—
woe and alas. *Help*, I yelled, *help*, as a joke
in the mighty din of metal upon metal. I sat
on the floor in the cool satellite cafeteria
across from a line of vending machines—
Twinkies and a Coke. Breakfast of Champions,
and wasn't I one, the scholar/bard of the plant
if anyone cared?

Hell? What did I know about it,
eating Twinkies in God's Holy Satellite? Nobody
cared. Not the guy I tripped who cursed
my idiot foot. Dante, Schmante, he might've said
as he stomped his steel-toed boot on mine.
That kind of says it all, Dante.
I never finished your book.

Laughing from Here

for all my brothers

We trudged over flat streets like old dogs who'd lost
the scent, though we were young and mostly

frisky. July 4, but we'd worked 12 factory hours.
Barbecues and beer ha-ha-ed out from cracked

twilight patios. Cement, the great magnifier, weight
of our flat globe, map of our legacy.

Dangling lunch pails clunked
hard against our thighs, our smart-ass wisdom.

At home, beers in the cooler with our names
on them. If we hurried. When we were kids

we fought to be first to shout
First on the streetlights! when they came on.

And that meant what? I don't know,
but I felt that way as we rounded the square

corner, and I turned and said,
I can hear dad laughing from here.

Room Divider

We had no room large enough
to divide, so it stood against the living
room wall where my father had knocked
down the boxy coat closet jutting out
like an abandoned confessional.
He'd swung his sledge into plaster, white dust
rising with the grit of forgiveness, fingerprints
dusting longneck bottles lined against the wall.

The room divider covered the bare wall
with the predictable reassurance of squares
displaying my mother's fake birds and their nests,
ceramic Madonnas or nativities, vases
of plastic flowers or antique Scout projects,
depending on the season.
We had two chairs, a lamp, and a TV.
Five kids sprawled on the floor, faces at the set,
waiting for somebody to make us
laugh, waiting to change the channel
or argue about it.

I cannot say why the room divider was purchased.
A mystery, like the half-set of encyclopedias
molding in the basement. If we'd had accomplishments
they would have been displayed there.
In the one drawer, we stored an atlas
that was never touched
and a candy jar that was.

Hard Candy

In a dented metal dish on her coffee table
my grandmother kept the bright-colored stones.
Summer heat clumped them. Christmas,
they rattled like the jewels of her hard red heart.

We took them—striped, round,
pillowed, swirled, square—regardless
of season or hunger. We sucked them small.
We did not choke. We sat and waited
for their sticky disappearance. She spit
on a hanky and wiped our faces
and said, *There, there.*

My father inherited the unspoken bitterness
of grief. He refused all sweets. He dropped us
off, he picked us up, he did not linger.
His brother and sister died young, children
forever, sealed in sticky silence.

My grandmother would rot our teeth away
before she'd say a thing. When we'd bite,
the crunch echoed off her pale pink walls.
She scolded. She had no teeth herself.
She wore the same dress every day of her life
according to my sources, who, it's true,
were distracted by candy.

Her humped back, buried eyes, deliberate
step—one big shell, and the candy,
little shells. The dish clicked closed
with the finality of bone. Once I found
a Tootsie Roll, but even that was petrified.

They lived across from St. Rose Church.
I dreamt my father and his siblings
at an upstairs window threw paper airplanes
across the street at God. Sending wishes,
I think. I could not read them, even in dream.

Once, before she died, she called me
by her dead son's name. The next time,
she called me doctor. Silence
was meant to be sweet and long lasting.

Catherine and Jack were their names.
Perhaps that's all they wrote on those planes
before letting them fly.

Last Meals

My mother's down to three meals
she can cook. Blind, she measures
with her fingers. Spills wash over
the counter, leavings of a bitter tide.

My father, allowed nothing green, must
have meat. Their dueling pills rattle off
sticky tile. Chicken tonight, dry breasts over rice.
Milk for their bones, dropped morsels for mice.

What can I do against their wiry will
to carry on? I recite with them remembered
grace. I clear the dishes—that's allowed.
TV and audio books muffle them into sleep—

on his couch, in her chair—and I am talking to
nothing but air. I eat the salt meant to be sugar.

WELCOME TO WARREN

Welcome to Warren

The Buy American City

I. The Exploding Cigar Tour

We snarl like dogs pacing against fences.

We love our fences—damn it, don't touch.

. . .

Want to look around, take the two-minute tour?

Or should we kick your ass now

and get it over with?

. . .

If you're looking for capital letters

you're shit out of luck

in this neighborhood.

. . .

The Land of Big Ideas

exists in a different tax bracket.

Big ideas sound like whining to us.

. . .

Take a number and wait your turn.

Time's got a lot on its hands.

The ticket has an expiration date.

That date has passed. Late fees due.

Numbers scrambled, runny

like bad eggs we're accused of being.

Why do our bosses put us in one basket

then drop the basket, then pat each other

on the back and say, *Well done*?

. . .

Our ice cream man was Mr. Softee,

not Mr. Lofty. He got busted

for selling pot not popsicles.

. . .

We used to make mud pies like everybody else

but we got over it.

If you've got a clear puddle

why add mud and stir it up

so nobody can see the bottom

then try to explain the benefits

of muddiness and half-muddiness

and theoretical muddiness?

Somebody around here's

gonna push you in the damn puddle.

That's understandable

in a lowercase way.

. . .

But some mornings, the sun is so sharp—

every brick and concrete angle blessed

with edge, light and shadow breaking

the world in two—even God

would approve, walking down the street

with his blindness stick

and feeling the light.

II. Around the Block

We celebrated the two places
where the sidewalk buckled.

Nobody could play drums.
Everyone pretended to play guitar.

No one had a nickname that took.
Like seeds in our poisoned dirt.

I dreamed of a piano only once.
I am uncertain of details.

My brother did a wheelie around the block
to widespread acclaim. He was offered
the body of a young virgin, and he took it.

Only one capital-V Virgin, constructed of auto scrap
and the holy spit of ancient welders.

A wide, sweeping turn around the bent
street sign, caught in a permanent lean.
It held up half a Bonneville coupe
from the land of Bonnies. From the isle
of electric sins and battery-operated priests.

We ate battery-acid oatmeal spiked with Tang
for good measure. We laughed in the surly face
of good measure.

I'm still standing on the corner waiting for you.
Or someone like you. Or someone
not like you at all. If you got 'em, smoke 'em.
If you don't got 'em, stick that in your pipe
and shove it up your ass and grab it by the balls
and piss it away. Life is a bowl of raw hamburger.

When the first gun clattered or clunked to the sidewalk,
sweet Jesus locked every front door on the block
and gave the key to his grandmother and told her
never under any circumstances to swallow the key
without his permission. That's how we ended up
studying her shit for something shiny.

We prayed for the evaporation of bullets,
but it was too late. In fact, the clocks had fallen
forward an hour just for spite. To give us more light
to stare at each other—half blame, half guilt.

And who was going to lick that spoon?
The engine wouldn't turn over.
It groaned and went back to sleep.

One big engine and 143 spark plugs.
One math book, nobody claiming it.
The story problem of our lives.
The breeze of air guitars conjuring
one long extended ache.

I'm on the corner of Rome and Bach
in front of what used to be
the Cryder house. The Semanski house.
The Semantics house. The house of Ill
Dispute and Domestic Repute. The Arab
house. The Indian house. The house
of Mean Dog Run and Funhouse Firearms.

I'm standing on the corner, shifting foot to foot,
leaning against a telephone pole pocked with tacks
from posters advertising lost dogs, just desserts,
but only if you eat your vegetables and crow.
I ran naked around the block past midnight
not once but twice. Falling star.

We spelled *decent* descent and stood
uncorrected. Undetected.
We were detectives for our own hearts.
We doodled the oblong shape
of that one block. We always closed the loop.

I'm the darker spot where you lingered
before picking up the pen.
Me, on the corner. Unerasable.
Half-erased. Creased. Frayed. Smudged
with a grudge. Hey. Hey. Look at me.
I'm calling your name.

III. Hidden Beauty

1.

If you have a map, eat it.

The old man wedging curb-grit under his nails

will give you directions for getting lost.

Getting off the grid involves talking in tongues

with other tongues. Follow the sidewalks

up to front doors and offer coupons

for eternal life. Faith involves

expiration dates and post-dated checks.

Take two stray dogs and call me in the morning.

I will not answer. I will be adjusting

the antenna on my personal savior.

2.

Do not fear that large square cinderblock building

into which we disappear. We call it

the fact-tree. Make sure you have

Hearing Protection, Eye Protection,

Sammich Protection, Automatic-Flush Protection,

Steel-Toe Protection. Skin Protection—

scrub away your life, or hope for a buyout.

Or a callback, depending. Echo Protection.

Obscene-Gesture Protection.

Tattoo Protection. Snow-Job protection.

Ass-kicking? You're on your own.

Smoking is good for you. Jesus got stitches

and is welding axle housings again. C'mon,

welcome him back with a man-hug.

3.

Chrysler Star: five thin points
of the splayed Jesus, the legs-spread
Jesus, the pagan Jesus itching
to get a word in edgewise
before someone else buys the company
just to turn it all into scrap metal
or a theme park for those nostalgic
for benefits and decent wages.

4.

Okay, I've led you around blind-
folded long enough. The beauty
of Warren, Michigan, lies under
the raised sidewalk square tilted
by underground root-shifting. Lift it up.
It's a door to Upsidedownville.
Someone will offer you a beer. Take it.
Someone will offer you a lawn chair,
a Cuban cigar from Canada,
and a million dollars. Ask them
about the weather. Ask them,
Working hard, or hardly working?

5.

It's time to take down one seasonal
display and erect another. And catch
the punk who burned *Fuck You*
into your lawn on Devil's Night.
It's your turn to be the Avenging Angel

of All Saints' Day and stone the villagers
for forgetting all the lies they'd memorized.
Take off your Upward Mobility mascot costume.
Take all your pennies to the bank.
Forget your pin number.
Stick a pin. Pull out the pin.
Ho ho ho, Halloween bunny!

6.

We can be holy when called upon.
Holier than thou and thou's monkey's uncle
and thou's you-and-what-army.

Once this guy took out his snowblower
and cleared everyone's sidewalk on the street.
He turned the corner, and we never saw him again
until he emerged on a new stamp
when the rates went up again.

7.

I almost forgot the ode to weed killer.
It goes something like this:
poison is good for me
poison will set me free
poison will reduce irony and age spots
God bless poison and all its many false antidotes
God bless lurid artificial green.

Nothing vague about it. Benefits visible.
Drawbacks slow-moving and inevitable
and almost as good as the mirages

of overtime and COL adjustments
and spinal adjustments and bitter
pills claiming good intentions.

8.
The Bible contradicts itself,
which is the best truth imaginable.
The Unwanted Pregnancy
of religious texts. Shotgun
conversions and deathbed blasphemies.
The one Good Christian has abandoned
the Candy Store for the 2-for-1 special
at the One-Stop Brothel next to the Tire Store,
the Shocks and Struts Store.

9.
This won't hurt. It'll just
kill you. On this church
I shall build my rock.
Upsidedownville is conducting
a recount, demanding the beer
and the chair, offering only
the Elusive Smirk in exchange.
We'd all be sitting here naked
if it wasn't so damn cold.

Maybe it's *three* stray dogs
and call me a *motherfucker*.

10.

Take a deep breath and count
to ten. Subtract the number
of years to retirement minus
the big layoff around the corner
and add your blood pressure and cholesterol.
If you have a will, eat it.
Tell the old man collecting curb dirt
you'll see him in hell.
Tell him to keep an eye on your family
while you're gone. The good eye,
not that other one. Scatter
your spare change to the wind
just to get a laugh from the neighbors
while the eight-year-old boy
hired specially for the occasion
gathers the coins, then shoots you
in the back so you free-fall directly
into the darkness beneath the sidewalk square
and it slams down on you like a coffin lid,
the old man smoothing fresh cement
so we can carve in the initials of the living
in the futile gesture of permanence
passed down by our fathers that, with a dollar,
might get us a cup of coffee
while we wait our turn
to name our poison.

IV. Legendary Parks*

The GM Tech Center sprawls across 330 acres of land and includes 11 miles of roads and 1.1 miles of tunnels. It includes 25 main buildings, a water tower, and 22-acre lake.

Mill Ends Park in Portland, Oregon, was created on St. Patrick's Day in 1948 to be a colony for leprechauns. The smallest park in the world, according to the Guinness Book of Records, is a circle 2 feet across in a traffic median.

The mad scientists on city council are concocting theories
on what constitutes a park—how tiny can it be?
While the Chrysler Truck Assembly Plant on Mound
occupies 87 acres, Shaw Park occupies a postage-stamp-sized field.
You can't even screw there without your feet dangling
into the street, and I've tried. Right, Lisa Likowski?
While the GM Tech Center, designed by Eero Saarinen
of crossword puzzle fame, occupies 390 acres and is rumored
to have its own lake, though only engineers who know
the secret handshake are allowed to view this lake,
and only with special goggles constructed out of windshield glass,

Shaw Park consists of concrete-block toilets always locked
for my safety and yours. The old tennis court turned
into a replica of the La Brea tar pits, fenced in
for my safety and yours. The rusted playground equipment
has been removed for my . . . yeah . . . You can't even get high
there anymore—
they cut down all the trees for . . . my safety and yours.

*Some of these facts are subject to a margin of error plus or minus 1,000,000, and the inclusion of outright lies, in the great American tradition, is taken for granted.

Excavation of the tennis courts has revealed an ancient burial ground
for bongs and empty Ripple bottles. The one bone found
turned out to be petrified dog shit from the world's largest Great Dane,
the dog of choice before the upturn in cute little pit bulls and Rottweilers.
Of course, now, no pets are allowed for . . .

The scientist-councilmen are busy trying to build a new tax base
for when the Big 3 go under. The duct tape-and-mirrors
experiments have so far proven to be inconclusive
disasters. Each house and lot in Warren, exactly the same size,
determined by a complex formula involving the square roots
of the one tree remaining in Shaw Park and the prime numbers
of public bathrooms that are actually open. Each house,
the size of a Strike Anywhere matchbox. Each match cut down
to size by the lack of civic imagination and economic piss-ability.

It is rumored some have escaped by digging through
their basements to China or Shangri-La or the mythical land
of Up North. The scientist-councilmen are testing ancient
cigarette butts and squirrel brains for clues. While Portland
makes jokes about the smallest park, our city council scientists
work on a very serious smaller park. They have the American
Can-Do Spirit. They drink cases of it at every meeting.
All in Good Fun, Idaho, is rumored to be working
on their own tiny park. Here in Warren, the Scouts
are holding a contest to see if it's possible to get lost
in a city park—the renegade Eagle Scout
arsonist has been disqualified.

The city fathers are working on creating the world's largest
merit badge to be installed in the world's smallest park.
"Fuck leprechauns" will be the slogan. Bumper stickers
are being printed up—the start of any good project in Warren,
the only city in America to try to construct a downtown
after the fact, a center where there is no center.
The new Seniors Center consists of one treadmill
and three defibrillators. For your safety and . . .
Each machine is named for a former mayor.
We love our local history here. The biggest Warren
in America. Our park will be a single blade
of grass drenched in toxic fertilizer.
The fence surrounding this blade
will be electrified.

V. The Heavy Stuff

We've moved the heavy stuff out of my parents' house
in Warren after 42 years, 7 months, and 23 days.

I had a good cry on the porch last night.
The picture window rattled in spring wind.

I kissed the cold porch light before turning in
to a child sleeping on the floor of my old room

my father built in the basement. Tomorrow,
it's their beds, and the light stuff,

the fragile, boxed, and labeled stuff.
If memory were a contest, the liars would win.

I've already lost the hole in the wall my ass made
at fifteen, drunk, falling to evade my mother's kiss.

Packing up the heavy stuff, we were startled
by a hawk crashing into that window, a small bird

in its mouth plucked from the feeder.
A hawk out of fucking nowhere. We always said

we lived in Fucking Nowhere, a community with no
center, no downtown. If it died, no one

could identify the body, though it's dying now,
the internal organs of factories and machine shops

darkening with despair. On the floor, I heard a train whistle
moan from the tracks near the Chrysler plant.

I thought of my grandfather pushing in the Off button
on his old b & w, dropping off to sleep, tiny star fading

from the screen. That TV now sits in my attic, miles
from this old house. Tomorrow I will drive home

to measure the new distance from their "tiny new digs" in remote
suburbia. I own that TV, but now I am getting another one,

Aunt Maureen's—my father'd kept it in the basement as a spare.
I own the TVs of two dead people and counting. TVs count

as heavy stuff. Before we moved my grandfather out
of his house, he'd kept three TVs, though only one worked—

to thwart burglars. We abandoned the other two. Perhaps
they still sit in that house no one would buy, abandoned

to weeds, guns, needles. The door swung open in the wind
last year when my father and I drove by.

The last standing house on a street of rubble.
They're probably not sleeping now, my parents,

behind the closed door. Though I hear

nothing. A hawk, can you believe it,

in Warren, Michigan? Old neighbors already gone,

having waved their limp good-byes years ago.

Yesterday, I sliced my finger with a box knife

and swallowed the blood. In the morning,

I'll dump the last of the birdseed in the yard,

knowing that hawk is out there.

VI. The End of Childhood

Fine dust in the summer field of childhood

and caved basements of lust

unfinished and forgotten feuds

vile taunts and singsong slurs.

The gentle stench of poisoned weeds

the absence of stately trees, adult supervision

wide, flat factories

and the chemical tar of their parking lots.

Gearless bicycles and greasy rags

and rolled-up T-shirts, the foreign tenderness

of girls we shied away from, then dreamt about.

It was never as simple as a cigarette tossed

from a passing car, soaring, then sparking

against the street, but I remember one night

standing on a corner, watching it land.

3

LATE INVOCATION FOR MAGIC

Late Invocation for Magic

In our box houses
on our cracked sidewalks
on our pockmarked streets
we scoffed at magic early on

and tormented anyone who didn't
until they sulked back into their dark
basements with their hidden-ball tricks,
their sleeves full of scarves.

We threw popcorn at the movie screens
of every kiss and happy ending.
We built plastic models of our favorite
monsters and made good use

of leftover glue. The only trick
was *here today, gone tomorrow,*
but we knew where everybody went,
the bigger box, the big black hat

of the factory no rabbits ever
emerged from. Nobody wore
a hat like that to begin with
in a neighborhood of good bullies

and bad. Our fathers cracked
their knuckles against our skulls.
It relieved tension. What was that game
where we just stood there punching

each other? The one where we jumped
randomly on one of our own
just for practice? If it's magic,
why would you have to practice?

Our fairy princesses got pregnant,
and their princes shrugged and abandoned them.
Our priests couldn't even get it up for Jesus,
and, thus, overcompensated.

. . .

A long time ago, yet still I'm choking
on the bitter fumes that scoffed
at the fancy gilt letters of faith
and any kindness not compensated

with cash. The colder and harder, the better—
the better the batter for silver-dollar
pancakes at the Clock diner Sunday morning
while mass droned on down the block.

There's a trick to get a stick shift
into reverse. One drunken midnight
my sister and I danced in the bed of a pickup
till the neighbors got out their guns

and shot us dead. We rose
from the dead rather quickly and without
ceremony or to-do. The neighbors
paused to reload, and we somersaulted
over the bushes like superheroes.

My brother bought a Jacuzzi with the settlement
from his motorcycle accident. Some teenager
ran a stop sign and sent him flying into the ER
from which he emerged much less certain

but one winter night he called me to ask
if it was snowing here too because it was
beautiful coming down on the steam
as he sat there in hot water admiring
his neighbor's controversial high fence.

Attitude, that's something we could wrap
our fists around. Takes attitude to build
a high stone fence against all codes
because you hate your neighbor.

C'mon, slap out of it. Every fairy tale
seems to end with the ogre getting his cut,
people looking back over their shoulders
even when the promised land beckons.

We drew a treasure map once, then found
something to bury. A dead dog, but we treated it
with due respect. You can't fix a magic wand
with duct tape and X-brand adhesive.

I miss those monsters—Ghidorah, Mothra,
Rodan, and the dapper master of ceremonies,
Godzilla. Then, the humans—Werewolf,
Dracula, Henry Ford. I loved painting
their tiny eyeballs.

Magic, magic, I keep repeating, on the path,
following the markers, trying to get there.
All of our wands turned out to be
sharp, pointy, and humorless.

The plan for this part was to be more
upbeat, to find an earned magic to believe in
and to celebrate the wispy colored scarves of dreams,
to hold hands in the street in a great kumbaya moment
or to at least stop smoking cigarettes.

The magic words were all advertising slogans
for companies that served as fronts for the mob.
Perhaps I exaggerate. We sawed each other
not in half, but down to size.

We had one girl on our street
who could sing all the high notes
and won all the talent contests.
I'll call her Marlene, though I could call

her anything now, dead these forty years.
Use your imagination. Close your eyes
and make a wish. Say the magic words.

Weeding Out the Weak

In dark slits between houses
　　only strong weeds grew.
Like stiff rags, spiked curses. Weeds

that spelled themselves in all caps, rising
　　from cracks, rubble, cold dirt.
Rough brick rose on either side, mortar crumbling

to dust, dust falling to earth, earth's bad breath
　　breeding sin. What better place for our first
kisses, frantic meeting of mouths open too wide,

mad tongues, gasping echoes of breath,
　　moist, toxic, nourishing? Or second kisses,
or third? Spiders told no lies, and weeds told

no secrets. Curious dogs sniffed our crotches
　　and moved on.

Letter to Andy

Do we give up on ever seeing each other again?
Today the envelope I sent your letter in
arrived back, having been delivered empty
to you. You returned it to sender, my words
lost to both of us, and I'm wondering—
just now, in my driveway, a robin picked up
a fat worm and tossed it in the air—wondering
if I have it in me to rewrite that letter.

When do we wad up the last letter, toss
it into the boxing ring like a bloody towel,
wave the red flag at the bull of—of—not history,
not death—time?—let it mow us down, gore us
with unfinished business, lush, fuzzy blankets
of what we imagine was happiness?

You know what the robin does to the worm.
I turn from the window. How's the bad back?
The bad knee? Our bodies losing
humor/goodness/consideration. Maybe
we should've gotten better tattoos and smoked
more cigarettes, eh, old friend?
But we both have mothers still alive,
so we're young, right? We've never
embraced, even at your father's funeral.

Weeds rise rampant in my garden—
maybe I can get one of the kids to pull them.
We live 383 miles apart. Perhaps we could meet
halfway at a rest stop in Ohio and reminisce about
the gory Ohio Highway Patrol driver's ed videos
over giant cups of weak coffee?

97° predicted today, and that worm
would've shriveled up on the driveway later
if it didn't get chopped and gobbled now.
Are those our options? Between shit and a hard place?

The morning after your father died in the front seat
while shattered sunglasses sliced your face in the back,
junior year—the morning after—I spotted you moving
down the street toward my house for us to walk
to school together like usual: *What's he doing*
going to school? What do I say?

Your face exed with stitches. I joined your silence
at the sidewalk. At school, some punk teased you
as if a girl cut you up. Third period, you left
to join your mother so crazed with grief she'd let you go.

Still alive—our mothers still alive. My father
still alive. Your stepfather gone, wheelchair crashed
down the steps at our old Catholic school
turned to Seniors Center. You know all this—

and my letter disappeared, and will
we see each other again and stop
the hungry robin doing its job?
Old friend, in lieu of meeting you halfway.
Old friend, I cowered at my front door.

Last month I shoveled a robin into a plastic bag
dead in the same driveway, proud cat
running wild next door. We've seen the cartoons,
but here in 3-D, the stench gagged me. Maggots
doing their maggot jobs. All we're sharing now
is this wave of heat.

In the funeral home, just you and your mother.
Your thick tie lumped your throat.
You studied your hands, and I studied mine,
but if we'd written answers there,
they'd washed away.

To escape your mother's sag and the shag
rug of that house where memory erased
itself into dust motes floating in the sun,
we outlined Detroit's industrial squares
in the party van bought with life insurance,
but your scars were fresh and the girls leery.

Maybe here's what I want to remember:
senior year, we drove to your house or mine
for lunch, spreading out sandwiches
in our empty houses, pouring milk
into our parents' glasses, away
from the cafeteria's mad clatter.

Like old men, survivors breaking bread—
peanut butter and jelly, apple or banana.
Just to be away from there—in a house
where nothing crashed, no one yelled
or screamed or dropped a thing.
If God was there, he was letting us be.

Like the old men we are now.
I cannot remember what I wrote.
If this is my last letter to you, remember
I said nothing.

The Monkees, 1968

We ran down Rome in Warren—
spitting distance from Eight Mile Road,
the Detroit border.
Hey, Hey,
we're the Monkees. Andy was short
and Davy. I was tall and goofy and Mike.
Our fathers built cars together, maybe
cracking dirty jokes and cheating
at cards in the lunchroom
like we'd be doing
soon enough. Maybe sharing a few choice words
about their black co-workers.
Like we'd be doing?
The smoky shadow of summer '67
still stung the air, but it was a new season.
New episodes. New hijinks.
New songs
to sing along to. *Hey, hey* . . . The street nearly empty.
Our fathers parked at the plant. Our mothers
buried inside boxy houses, maybe smoking cigs
and boiling spaghetti water. Maybe waiting
for the party line to clear, maybe waiting
for the absent applause.
What happened
on the other side of Eight Mile wasn't on TV
except for the news, but we weren't watching.
Our channels were limited to a few square blocks,

one square TV screen, and maybe we were in love.

12, 13. December, 1968. No Mickey, no Peter.

Snow clean enough to eat if we hurried.

Kicking it up where it blew back in our faces

and we laughed

                    and sang loud, louder

but the snow muffled our changing

voices. We did not know the Monkees

couldn't play their own instruments

or why black people were angry.

Black-and-white TV. The casual

they and *we* of the border

                                        forever burned away

by one hot summer. But we didn't know what

they sang over there. 12. 13. The camera zoomed in:

we posed, we danced. No one out in that swirl of snow

to make fun of us. To call us by our real names.

"School's Out," Alice Cooper, 1972

The original album cover had the sleeve opening in the manner of an old school desk. The vinyl record inside was wrapped in a pair of girl's panties. This original issue was recalled because the panties were not flame-retardant.

Alice knew what I wanted:
black vinyl sheathed in sky-blue panties
I hid in my dresser. My mother found them—
threw them out without a word. Panties!

In my tiny room on the edge of Detroit, black light
glowed on the frayed posters of my minor gods.
I counted the girls I'd kissed, then multiplied
with lust. I fingered the cheap elastic band
and erupted in my sleep.

Alice's desk: marbles, slingshot, jackknife.
Scratched initials, stuck gum.
Mine: plastic sheet soured with lunch milk,
three gnawed pencils, one hard pink eraser.

A guy named Alice with the face
of cartoon death. Surly mascara barked
from the coffins of my speakers.
The song blew up school. School as prison—
a metaphor made quaint by factories
in our future that offered no graduation.

Lifer, I'd call myself, as my father did.

Afternoon shift. Black vinyl circling midnights.

In headphones, *School's out forever.*

I drifted to the sounds of simulated

damage and counted my hours of overtime

then multiplied myself to sleep.

Flame retardant.

Collector's items now, those panties.

Infamous

breaks the pattern of pre-
fixes and suffixes not taking
the stress:
[in-fuh-muhs]

which makes me think:
muh-fuhs
as in what you muh-fuhs
lookin at?

which could have been an infamous
last question, given
that those muh-fuhs
stared at me all hard-rocky

and took a few steps till I broke
into a shit-teeth grin
saying, *Aw, go ahead,*
look all you like.

She—see, they wuz lookin at
us fighting, she and me, and she—
how many witnesses do you need
to call it infamous?—

she sez, *What YOU lookin at*
when I look at her
with my scarecrow shrug
while my Greek chorus

on the street howls and hoots
waving tattoos and gang signs
in a patriotic display

and she gets in the car and waits
for her last ride home from me—
we didn't even finish the fight.

An infamous quote can be one
where you predict the future
and you're dead dry-bone wrong

so when I dropped her off and said,
See ya later, the door slammed behind her,
whiplashing my words right back at me.

Where's the chorus when you need them?
Back on that corner miles away
near the bad movie of our fight—
thumbs down, no stars, bomb, bomb, bomb,

or so I imagine, my Bible of Shame
burning in my hands like a bush, talking
in the tongues of the infamous.

The Unpregnant Pause

This is a short story interrupted to make it
shorter: Penny babysat across the street
for the British divorcee maniacally cheerful
driving off with her date.

She came home early—us half-naked, fully entangled
on her bed. I barged into the bathroom. Penny stumbled
out to greet her. Penny'd wanted to do it that night.
Six months later, with Laffy Rodgers, she did.

I never saw the British woman again.
She'd smiled at me when I finally emerged
half-together, half-apart. She was half
moved in, half out. We shouldn't have used her bed.

I have the nostalgia of a soldier who got stationed
stateside during the war. Penny had good intentions—
all those potholes on the way to hell.

Her head shook as if the earth was moving,
and of course it was. But we can't *make* the earth
move. The earth does what it does. Good-bye, British lady!
Good-bye British lady's toddler, Donald!

Good-bye Penny and Penny's baby and Laffy,
proud papa dutifully dropping out
to sell drugs full-time. I have the nostalgia
of the mouse biting off its tail to escape the trap

which is no nostalgia at all, given the cheese
is untasted. This is the long version of a short story.
Sometimes an interruption lasts forever.
The British lady didn't care.

Perhaps she'd just had sex herself. But what happened
to bring her back so quick? What took me so long
in the bathroom? Was it the rest of my life steaming
the mirror, British lady?

Some nights, even now, I hear her car in the driveway.
Penny and I broke up after I was robbed at gunpoint
working at the corner store. I started smoking
and quit smoking. *Laffy, she's all yours, pal,*

I choked out, his hands pliered around my neck.
How'd he get a name like that?
I accepted on faith that the gun was loaded,
that all guns are loaded.

Throw me in the back of a speeding car and drive past
their old houses. Squeal the tires. Don't hit the ghosts.
Is the road to heaven paved with bad intentions?
The referee's out in the parking lot getting half-

loaded before the game, his judgment partly cloudy
with a chance of showers. The road to sex isn't paved at all.
The toll taker shows up in unexpected locations
demanding exact change.

I could've been Laffy in the wink of the eye of the queen,
for I didn't know jack-shit except the urge to quiver
and that doesn't count as knowledge
according to our semi-referee.

I have the nostalgia of a gravestone before it's carved,
the nostalgia of an ancient immigrant for an accent,
the nostalgia of a dog for the birthday cake
it once devoured, then got sick on.

I have the nostalgia of the jailed drug dealer—shout out
to you, Laffy! Last I heard, last I heard . . . Like that road
turned to trail, turned to brush, so here it ends, surrounded
by the vines and tangles of my own sweet jungle.

Calling Out Marlene Miller

She died in a freak fire—spilled gas
caught on the drier pilot. Thirteen,
we'd been heading toward high-school cool.
If we had ants in our pants, they clustered.
We sure itched to take them off
and run naked around the block—
and did one night that summer.

Some of us already had funeral black to wear.
We dared each other to approach the coffin
like it was some super-duper high dive.
We were supposed to whisper a prayer,
but we'd just stopped praying
and weren't ready yet to start up again,
but we couldn't just say, *Hey* or *See ya*.

In the parking lot, squinting through
Kools and Marlboros, we couldn't tell
funny stories about her, or look past our own
thin shadows. Frank and Eddie argued
over whether the song went "God Loves Rock 'n' Roll"
or "God, Love, and Rock 'n' Roll." Bill sniffed
smelling salts he'd lifted, and his eyebrows
disappeared. Someone had switched our lives
to reverse, and we couldn't decode the secret lyrics.

Hey Marlene, remember that time you
gave me a hickie? Remember that time
I snapped your bra strap? Hey,
Marlene, remember our swollen lips
after we'd kissed all night in the empty garage?
Hey Marlene, remember when I rode you
on my bike down to the corner store
and we ate red popsicles and laughed at
each other's clown faces and you grabbed
my waist as we rode over a bump,
how you screamed and laughed?

Hey—Marlene.

Dead Girl

After the fire, Kim and I held hands
on her swing and blew sad bubbles
for our dead friend. I flinched at her
black mascara lined with blue sparkles.

The firemen's ladders clanked off gutters.
The air stank with dead smoke, burned
rubber before a crash.
The dead girl had kissed my neck.
I'd tilted my head to give her room.

Kim dropped out to dance at the Cricket.
Her makeup did not run as we pushed off
and swayed on the swing. I shed
no tears myself, but winced against
her cigarette and pushed hard against dirt.

Marlene was the dead girl's name.
My parents called her the Dead Girl.
Kim danced at the Cricket then disappeared.
I had held her hand once, and we'd grieved.

Yes, I saw her there.
I clapped and hooted.

Homemade Prom Dress

She's looking at the 5x7 she once kept
beside her bed. In Home Ec, she'd
sewn the bold blue flowered thing
from curtains. She got an A—
though, dropping out, it did not matter.

Lipstick, blaring-sweet maraschino red dye #2,
lethal in large doses. She knew no small doses,
her mother's dyed Russian frizz fussing over her
as she sweat into yellow flowers under her arms
for the Great American Prom.

In a hall walled with blood-red fuzz,
she was the girl with the homemade dress
that everybody knew would not be on her long.
He swigged and swizzled from a silver flask.

He drove reckless and wrecked
but did not crash. She was of two minds
when it was mindless she was after.
Red flower. Her smile, pure grit. Her laugh,
shrill, off the charts. Nobody crashed,
nobody died.

She took off her shoes in the motel room—
he lifted the dress over her head.
She wanted something that wasn't trite—
the other girls in their prefab poofy gowns.
She was an alien from a planet
resembling Hawaii where her mother

had once been queen. Until the king
abdicated, the king said,
I'm sorry sweetheart but I gotta go
and didn't send a goddamn dollar bill,
Christmas card, or valentine—
Christmas card or valentine.

Maybe her father ended up in prison
like him, the cocky boy behind the curtains
who she almost thought she loved.
He wasn't like her father, she said.
She didn't get pregnant to be
like her mother, she said.

She'd sewn her own damn dress
and who else did that?
The other Home Ec girls may as well
have been sewing their habits for the convent,
as likely as they were to get a prom date,
and the poofy chiffon crowd
delicately shunned her.

Flowers damp with moisture
on the bright blue sea. Breasts and hips,
the waves, the current. One bad boy
with a leaky boat looking for someone
to blame. He already had his gun
and two years later, he used it.

He wrote her from prison. She never
wrote back. So why should she
tell her story to some girl claiming
to be her daughter, wanting to meet
her *birth mother*—some novelty,
a story to tell? She didn't take chances
like that—risk having her story mocked.

She does not agree to meet, to talk,
to exchange letters. On the back
of the photo, she scrawls,
I made the dress myself.

FOE: Forwarding Order Expired

Gina Fiore lifted her dress to display
her hysterectomy scar. In their tiny kitchen,
her son, my friend Tony, turned away.
Thick red wine in a jug on the floor,
syrup for her brash rage.

Electroshock zapped nothing out of her
except a few extra cuss words.
Every Fiore twitched or flinched.
Who hit who? She might've lost track,
the short-fuse blows, the explosion's
numbing buzz, the deep grind
of an adult waiting for you to do
as you're told. You never knew whether a laugh
was coming—magenta streak of lip and tongue—
or the lower register of black gas, greasy smack.

We played her Redd Foxx LPs in their basement,
recorded live in some nightclub on Planet Sin,
the black circle crackling crass laughter.
Records *click*, *click*, and somebody's got to lift
the tone arm. Somebody's got to show us scars,
teach us the currency of double X.

Gina Fiore, the only adult to call Crazy Carl
Crazy. Hysterical bee, bent stinger, amplified
buzz. No telling it straight when she's wearing
a tiny gold metal-flake bikini, blushing up the mailman.
The only mother I could imagine enjoying sex,
her face orgasmically elastic, chewing large gum.
She had the heart of an urban lion
and the body of an aging porn star.

After divorcing Big Tony, who made deliveries
to the dark side of the coin, she showed up
in coveralls in the Ford plant, gray and gaunt
without makeup. She lasted twenty years there.

Gina Fiore, a wiggly exclamation point
ready to yank herself straight
in an instant. I loved her in pink silence
as she bent to wash her feet
before getting in the pool.
Gold metal-flake bikini!

I saw the moon landing on her TV.
Five minutes, then she clicked it off.
Bullshit, she said, *you'll see*.

Last time I saw her she was circling the block,
her feet shuffling two gritty sparks,
walking with Mrs. Miller, whose daughter
Marlene gave me my first true kiss before dying
in a basement fire. One long squealing tire.
One black record and a million blue jokes.

I should've said, *Hey Mrs. F, remember Redd Foxx*?
And, *Hey Mrs. Miller, I loved your daughter.*
They're bundled against it—the cold, death, whatever.
My breath rises here on the same porch
where Tony told me Marlene was dead
and I dove my tears into prickly bushes.

Osteoporosis, and she knows how to spell it,
leaning on Mrs. Miller as they pass.
My heart thick with grief's metal-flake.

Remember the one about the horse race,
the one about the blind man,
the one about, one about . . .

When Gina Fiore retired, she gave my father
a wet good-bye kiss at the plant. Bought a Fiesta
and drove to Florida for her bones, her crumbling bones,
never to be heard from again except in Christmas cards
to my mother, who kept her secrets.

Once I knocked an apple into one
of their pool table pockets. She cursed
the bad apple instead of me. The bad apple stuck.
Half-eaten. I could've used just one more bite.

The Garden of the Basement of Redd Foxx
and the apple of the scar and the blessed
holy waters of the backyard pool.

She worked in Heat Treat in the plant,
abandoning bikini lines to the greasy repetition
of loud, dull records.

That Fiesta's not rusting out
down in Florida outside the cute little trailer
she's got all decorated. When she moved,
Tony took what she left to the curb.
If I was there, I would have picked through it.
Maybe I just did.

Marlene, see what you missed, girl,
dying on us? Basements are for ghosts
so what's the big idea, dying there?
All you missed was the survival
of the rest of us, to be continued.
That red mark you left on my neck—
Gina Fiore laughed when she saw it,
then touched it gently with one long finger.

Isn't that as good a period as anything?

ECONOMIC FAIRY TALE

Soft Side of the Moon

City-heat concrete. No mercy or memory.
No give. Take. Night simmers fear, stirs.

Results offer no surprises:
Body count. Shrug. Aftertaste. Cringe

outstays its welcome. Trust lands belly-up
on the curb. Ask the mayor if he knows

where your street is and why they never pave it,
why they just patch the potholes one more time

and get the hell out of there. Hell that cannot be
patched over, blended, or mended.

Apostrophes of sweat. Inconsiderate sigh
hot in your face. Face to face over drugs

to spiral up and out. The mayor
has free tickets. Good seats. The mayor

is gelling his hair and fucking
the sacrificial virgin. On your corner

a woman on her knees for twenty.
The moon nostalgic for mis-

directed prayers and sincere propositions,
tired of the odd bargaining of the damned.

City-heat concrete puts your life in parentheses,
your smile in a life jacket, your head in the yoke

of straight-ahead-no-eye-contact. You have
a few things to say to the mayor

but he's established a hotline
to fry your phone calls. City council

sues each other over who has to pay
whose lawyers.

Talk radio has all the answers.
Even the moon is booing.

City-heat concrete. August taking
an illegal extension on the back end,

off the books. The Fan Man recites
rhyming couplets while AC salesmen
scat in their ice-powered suits.
Listen tonight to who backs down

and who simply goes down
and who simply stays down

and who rises again. City fault lines
go unpaved, unexamined, glued over

with spit and bribes.
The guy with the knife is just lonely.

The guy with the gun is just having
a bad day with Despair and her children.

And you, you're waiting for it to cool down.
You've got a hard-on for the moon

and a running battle with the dollar bill.
If only the police would stop by tonight

to brush your hair and pat you on the ass
maybe you could visit your old friend Sleep

living in a cool basement somewhere
on the other side of the moon.

Painting a Picture with Broken Crayons

Forty percent of the city's 88,000 streetlights are broken,
and the city, whose finances are overseen by an
appointed board, can't afford to fix them.

I'm digging my fingernails in to scrape
off more of the Crayola paper.
My palette consists of black and white.
Neither shows up on my canvas—
yesterday's newspaper printed
on cement slabs in invisible ink.

But that's a street-corner
caricature drawn by a clown
to attract customers, a ball
of ash for a nose, good
for a laugh, a buck or two.
The true story is revealed only
when the streetlights come on.
Close your eyes. Imagine.

Crayola Trailer Park Eight-Pack

Smudge: brownish blackish
bass guitarish. Point dulled permanent.

Bruise: bluish purple yellow
regret. Stains clothing, stains skin.

Stall: orange-ish greenish semi-drip.
Toxic to small animals, bored toddlers.

Clash: red shouted swirl. Surprising.
Deadly. Both draws and disperses crowds.

Grimace: dirty pink. Glass shards.
Odor disorder.

Static: tarnished silver purple splash.
Mix with speech to create sirens.

Witness: yellow laced with thin red lines.
Apply with eager silence.

Prayer: subtle opaque blue murmur.
Creates mirages. Erases as it goes.

The St. Vitus Dance of the Factory Floor

When thrown into the den of a hungry lion, the beast merely licked Vitus affectionately. . . . Some sixteenth-century Germans believed they could obtain a year's good health by dancing before the statue of St. Vitus on his feast day.

Ed in Dept. 53 painted gold foot-
prints on the factory floor
around his machine—a dance-step
pattern to keep him clean
while welding brake-line clips
onto axle housings.

He wore button-down shirts,
slacks, and the steel-toed
dress shoes of management.
Midnights—the foreman cared not.
Spotless Ed, poster boy
for Good Attitude
though it earned him
no more money
and less good will.

Why did we paint over
those footprints one night
when he was out sick?
We cupped our hands
around the dark candle
of cruelty in the dank swirl,
the sharp steel clamor.

The next day, we punched in
early to watch his wax face
melt into the numb stare
of the rest of us.

Rouge Overpass

You shouldn't be able to smell your work from
where you live.

Yellow smoke rises to the right,
gray smoke to the left. Incense
for the holy sacrament of the dollar bill.

On the paved river, Jesus drives
his big boat. We pinch our noses
at the smell of his decomposing body

or maybe we don't, depending
on our vestments, depending
on our chosen exits, depending on
the names of our saints.

Easter Sunday at Hakim's Convenience

Some mangy dog craps on the tree out front—
a pine that some punk's going to cut down and decorate
next Christmas, and then Hakim's really going to be pissed—
What's with you Christians and your holidays,
he wants to know, *rabbits, colored eggs,*
who damn dream that?
                                        I'm buying malted milk eggs
at half price, so he's assuming I can explain.
Hakim's, the only open store I can walk to.
Jesus Christ is risen today, allelu-allelu-alleloo-hoo-ya!
He knows I'm from the neighborhood and my kids
like blue popsicles and we drink 1% milk and request
a bag 99% of the time.
                                        His bags are pre-used but he still
doesn't like giving them up. I'm going to gorge on those eggs
till I'm just a little sick. Why I'm alone on Easter
we're not going into just now. I've got exact change.
Church across the street's spilling out
                                                            its Easter finery
into a gray spring Sunday. I don't know anything
about Hakim, another in the long line of hard men
trying to make a go of it in the old Uni-Mart
or its ten other names—Stop-n-Go, Minimart, 7-Eleven . . .
Mini and Uni fight it out on competing signs out front.
Hakim hasn't been shot. He carries more porn than the last guy.
Less groceries. I buy my Drano here. Hakim doubles
the price because *convenience*. I buy more Drano

than I should need. What's going on in those pipes?
Across the street, beautiful smiling faces
do the tulip dance in their bright duds.
Looking over here
                              at me and Hakim,
thinking—thinking what?—probably nothing. Nothing
like pity, in any case. And we don't want it.
Hakim wants dollars and I want eggs. Malted milk,
hmmm-mmmm.
                              We nodded greetings when I stepped in,
but as I step out, nobody's saying, *See ya* or *Later*.
Oh Lord, I mumble, chocolate running down
my chin, torn plastic in my hands, *come on back*.

Something Like a Sonnet for Something Like Peace

In high school, I lusted after the jagged cruelty of spray paint,
anonymous
slander of the foreign. Today, I lust after Hakim's meats sizzling
on the grill
chained to the fence outside his tiny store. For a morsel dropped
from Hakim's tongs into my open hands, I offer up my stopped
wristwatch

and a pack of matches from my brother's first wedding in 1973
after Nixon
abolished the draft. If God exists, would he want capital letters?
Would he
let anyone stumbling or strutting down the streets of this
cracked city
determine his will, steal this grill? Today I abandon the smudged
newsprint

of blood and the gnashing curses muted into polite musings. I
once lusted
after somebody else's prayers. I remain in fear's limbo. Today I'm
chewing
the holy meat on the street in September sun, juice running
down my chin.
I share a silent nod with Hakim. Above the clicking of meters
counting out

greed, above the cacophonic brass of cars on the boulevard,
I hear the wind chimes of the neighborhood stutterer.

July 20 Fireworks During Ongoing Conflicts Abroad

Two weeks after the Fourth, and they're still at it.
Rocket-sizzle and fizzle from apartment balconies
exploding into shredded curses above the street.

. . .

My friend Sam moved out when his downstairs
neighbor shot a bullet through the ceiling
that stuck in the wall of his son's room.

. . .

The distance to Baghdad or Kandahar
is measured in rowboat coffins
while here in the fatty palm of the Mitten
minor skirmishes electrify tedium.

. . .

The list of Frequently Asked Questions
has been shot into a crooked orbit
and may collide with logic in five thousand years.
The eye of the fuse is eternal.

. . .

Every explosion broadcasts a blatant lie.
I lay awake, shame-soaked sweat,
unable to dream the unimaginable.

. . .

If a rocket lands on my roof,
should I fire back?
Or should I shout up to the balcony,
try to talk things over?

Is talking things over
a quaint euphemism for failure?

. . .

They call them fatigues,
but they don't look tired.
Why not call them targets?

I'd like to read the label
on the juice they're drinking
and have it translated
into peaceful discourse.

. . .

The gentlemen across the street
bark after each explosion,
and the terrified dogs below
go silent.

. . .

Demonizing is an inexpensive
proposition, initially.
Pretty soon everybody's admiring
each other's pointy horns.

. . .

Shredded estimates of casualties
flutter to the ground, nearly indistinguishable
from the detritus of our city streets.

. . .

I can't call the police—
they'll want to meet outside
where armed insurgents can identify me.

I've been saying for days
that they'll run out of ammo soon.
Or simply tire of the identical explosions.
Or maybe we'll all just go deaf.

. . .

I can't even spell Baghdad. What's that h
doing there? Don't you think we need to know
how to spell before invading?

Our collective shrug starts to resemble
a sexy new dance.

. . .

I don't have the authority to complain
about fireworks, now legal in our state.

I don't know anyone who's died
in the distant Over There.
When I objected, my representative sent
a polite computerized response thanking me
for my input. When I marched,
the cops said, *Keep moving.*

. . .

Options are limited for the young men
across the street packed into tiny apartments,
sleeping on the floor, second-string drug dealers.

They may be signing up soon
to see the world with steady pay
and the right to kill.

. . .

Okay, that's a little harsh. Maybe they're just kids
playing boom-boom. Dying's a right too.

That apartment building, a house of cards
taller than my house of cards.

Light 'em if you've got 'em.
My sheets twist a-tangle
in localized fury and generalized despair.

. . .

July 20. The rest of us in our beds
roll over, yank pillows over our ears,
breath rising invisible in thick night air,
ownership impossible, grief abstract,
news underlined in invisible blood.

The boom of our hearts—
beating, shredding.

Quitting the Day Job in the Middle Ages

I have no day job. The alarm
is a harmonica. Hope for the hard

of hearing. Awake this morning and wishing
for background vocals. Call

and response. Cereal with fresh fruit
and saxophones in my coffee.

Newspaper curls and fades
in my fingers, somebody slamming on

the time accelerator, and it's not me.
Downsized into the backside of the slip-

and-slide. Benefits? The fish wrapped
in newspaper, fresh as last week's lie

about prior experience. Either
whap me with a ping-pong paddle

or peel an onion for me,
I don't really care. The old house

melts around me or gets shrink-
wrapped, I can't decide.

Outside, August waits. They say
it's hot and humid in Washington,

but they never sweat on TV.
Here in the Rust Belt of the Flyover States

I fill out my forms, press hard
on my memorized numbers.

That sound you hear is either
the sound of the drain sucking down

the last bit of moisture
or milk telling lies to my cereal.

A Game Called Rock

On my hands and knees, I arch
into a large boulder. My children climb up,
slide down. A good game when I am tired.

When my wife was mugged one night
walking up our driveway after waitressing,
her tips spilled, clinking down cracked cement,

a spray of angry bells. I installed decorative
bars on the windows and floodlights with sensors.
My children and I play Red Light/Green Light.

Ski Slope—they dive over bent knees
and land in the soft powder of my chest.
My wife dreams of moving someplace

safe, or even just quiet. Winters are better.
If we can survive another summer.
Coins roll down the driveway

and dollar bills drift out the open window.
Across the street, a car idles for drugs,
thumping its smoked bass. I push in

3-D Hyperbass Sound on my boom box—
at least it's *my* heart beating.

Christmas Dinner, 2008

The third-generation furniture upholsterer
has a kink in his neck. He splurges on pizza
for his old friends. His wife burned
the cookies, but they're on the table.

The GM draftsman on extended vacation
steals from the college fund and worries
his enormous weight into the bad back
of everything. Their church laid off the minister

then disbanded. The copywriter
who lost her hearing due to chemo
just laid off half her staff. She falls asleep
before the pizza arrives.

The upholsterer weighs a move
into the garage versus bankruptcy
and his mad father who never saved
for retirement and his mad brother

out of prison again. Ho ho ho,
America! Cheers! The kids sit sober
on the couch, even the teenagers
half-getting the message

that we're screwed. *Nice couch,*
one of them says. They eat
all the burned cookies.

Economic Fairy Tale: The Cement House

The wolf threw cigarette butts
against the wall and stomped off,
but the banker's bazooka full
of shiny new pennies blew
the roof offa the sucka. Rain
blurred the ink on the contract
that read *leave us alone*
and the doctor's prescription
when decoded by people
just doing their job
read *shit out of luck*. So,
mama and papa and baby too
rose into heaven above
the four concrete walls
or sank into the foundation
of what would soon become
a factory of wolves making
sheep's clothing, depending
on who you're listening to
if you're listening at all.

Yeah, I mean you,
with your toy shovel,
your wet matches,
your lucky penny.

Fifth of July: The Morning After with Lady Liberty

I dreamed the Statue of Liberty was giving the finger. Maybe just to me, I can't be sure in the already fading Dreamville photo—oh Sepia Smithers, my old true love, is that you in that mad green dress, still pissed off? Or maybe it's something heavier—some grand political statement, subtlety eroded by salt water or tears or nostalgia or designer footwear? I anticipated having nightmares about the Old-Men Oompah Band strutting in the square with their gigantic Uncle Sam hats. I don't remember Uncle S. having that enormous beer gut, but hey, Joey "Jaws" Chestnut ate 69 hot dogs in ten minutes yesterday. Why would *Joey Chestnut* need a nickname? Why would you eat 69 hot dogs? Why are you on the *sports* news? I met a famous weatherman yesterday and did not recognize him. Only in America, right, what's-her-name with the perfect hair? Oh Sepia, my long-lost Lady Liberty, why are you giving us all the finger, all of us in the harbor of American dreams? Who decided there's only one American Dream? The second American Dream is that Statue giving the finger. Out here in the Midwest we sweat like pigs over our grills and cook up pig parts and talk about Joey Chestnut: Ain't that sumpin? Yeah, sure is sumpin. Crazy Mother Fucker, that Joey Chestnut. The first t is silent. Speak up T, Mr. T, eating crazy like that. I like your big sparkly red-white-and-blue motherfucking hat, by the way. And I like yours as well, Mr. Monkey's Uncle. You ever get spit on by a monkey? Sure, plenty of times. Wouldn't you spit on people, locked up like that? Nah, it's a kind of monkey foreplay. Hey, you won't guess who I ran into in the supermarket last week—Sepia Smithers, and man, she's still got it going on, know what I mean? I'm sure you do. Remember that mad green dress? I surely do. Those French people, they crazy motherfuckers too. They don't even make hot dogs in France. What they cook on the Fourth of July? Would a monkey spit at the Statue of Liberty, or throw shit at it like the gorilla do? I wet my finger and hold it up to the wind, but there ain't no wind blowin' no which way. In my dream I'm giving the finger back, is what I've been meaning to say, a little exchange between old friends. The French got their own fucking holiday, you asshole. I'm thinking about Joey Chestnut sitting on the toilet—you think he like chestnuts? How about those toilets over there, they just holes in the ground, right? This whole time no fireworks going off. You know why? They'd wake me up from the dream! You gotta take a boat out just to talk to the lady, you believe that? Ain't no boat strong enough get you out to Sepia, dude. What I'm saying here is, why don't we talk anymore, Lady L? Don't your arm get tired holding up your finger? Why you got to be like that?

Summer Weight, Labor Day

The scale wavers its numbers
with the sagging burden
of mandated good times,
the hefty smoke of meat
on the stick, or off.

If earlier the calendar had blocked off
a week or two for vacation,
the postcards now thicken into bricks
and the peeled skin of sunburn erodes
into the cool dust of submission
and the list of chores dwindles
into dried paint under your nails.

Anticipation is a dog that's already
been kicked. Sad September.
If only you could go back
to school and do it right this time,
or merely better.

Pencils sharpened by August heat.
Lawn mowers on the prowl, fat drip
of gasoline stinging the air with fake nostalgia.
Sunday's a tepid ballgame in a lost season.

Monday is simple cruelty, the wallowing
before the storm. Children dance under streetlights
with the doomed grace of fireflies.
Oh, they don't know who's got it in for them yet,
barefoot, heading toward broken glass.

Zoom in on you sprawled on your porch
issuing lame challenges to insects and sunshine
to linger. Over a warm beer, you dream
of the perfect cool hat that could've
changed your life.

Crooked Teeth

My old friend Eddie grins his crooked teeth
when we meet outside his car
in the old neighborhood
I'm driving through *just because*
and he's living in his parents' old house
because he can and must.
Where better to meet in the Motor City
than outside our cars? Old cars, old teeth.
Long time, no seek.

Pull over, grab a beer. Look under his hood.
Tell a dirty joke. Wipe crud on a dirty rag.
Oil drip of nostalgia, black on the street.
Signature. Salutation. Soup-can tail pipe
and a wire hanger. Jesus and his
lost, greasy sheep. Divorced? Laid
off? Kids? Crooked smile. Insurance?
Crooked now, crooked then. Nobody
taking measurements or glamour shots.

Toothpick. The joke of savings.
The red cape of retirement. The blue
coveralls of this very moment, old
friend. Parents dead. House paid off.
Lord have mercy. Socket set. Knuckle-
scrape, knucklehead. Rusty bolt un-
stuck. Hand me that beer, Mr. Fixit.

King for a day, crown atilt.

Give it some gas. The kingdom turns

over. Nobody prettying up

that smile.

Homeless Arisen from Dead

Next to the river trail on a park bench
exposed to wind, snow, and forces of evil,
a bundle of lumped blankets spread open
to reveal, as I run closer, the absence of life.

A cold desperado in my protective face mask,
I'm getting fit for the new year. Wet snow tells
that old homeless story you're tired of hearing,
sentimental and calculating both.

Where did Jesus go? Taking a leak? Off getting
warm? Or is it Lazarus, scrounging in the dumpsters?
I shiver, happy not to find anyone, crusty with cruelty
or ice. Plastic bags under the bench. Rags.

A lousy spot, even given limited options. How about
under that overpass behind the bushes? What do I know,
in my desperado face mask, huffing down the icy lane
in cushioned sneakers and matching sweats?

No ID or spare change. Anonymous workout artist
discovers the resurrection and continues on.
To find the crown of thorns and the thirty pieces of silver.
Is happiness at what's unseen

true happiness, or the absence of?

Philosophy's not my strong suit.

My strong suit is back at the house.

The soiled blankets peeled back,

frosted petals of a ruined rose,

the rose sniffed by St. Thomas,

blood on his fingers as they emerged.

Me, I've got miles to go.

About the Author

Jim Daniels's recent books include *Apology to the Moon*, *Birth Marks*, and *Eight Mile High* (stories). He is also the writer/producer of a number of short films, including *The End of Blessings*. Born in Detroit, Daniels is the Thomas Stockham Baker University Professor at Carnegie Mellon University.